PATHWAY OF FIRE

PATHWAY OF

FIRE

Initiation to the Kabbalah

RAPHAEL

SAMUEL WEISER, INC.

York Beach, Maine

First published in 1993 by
Samuel Weiser, Inc.
Box 612
York Beach, Maine 03910

Library of Congress Cataloging-in-Publication Data

Raphael.
   Pathway of Fire : initiation to the Kabbalah / by Raphael.
      p. cm.
   Includes index.
       1. Cabala--Miscellanea.   2. Judaism--Relations--Hinduism--Miscellanea.   3. Hinduism--Relations--Judaism--Miscellanea.
   I. Title
   BM526.R35   1993
   296.1'6--dc20   92-44502
                                                  CIP

ISBN 0-87728-771-6
MG

Typeset in 11 point Palatino

Printed in the United States of America

The paper used in this publication meets the minimum requirements of the American National Standard for Permanence of Paper for Printed Library Materials Z39.48-1984

Table of Contents

Understand and you will know . . . . Ten Sephiroth, except the Ineffable, their end is joined with their beginning like the flame with the burning coal, only the Lord is above them and has no second.

———*Sepher Yezirah*

Foreword

The Hebrew term *Kabbalah* means "reception," "transmission," is equivalent to the word *Masorah*, and represents the esoteric part of the Old Testament. This means that the latter, besides having an exterior and outward function, has also got a deeper and significant one which is interior and esoteric.

In *Pirke Aboth I:1* of the Talmud we read:

"Moses received the Law (Torah) upon Mount Sinai and transmitted it to Joshua, Joshua transmitted it to the Elders, the Elders to the Prophets and the Prophets to the Great Congregation."

Thus, Moses is the first link in the chain of the kabbalistic tradition which "received" the *Masorah* from the divine Voice-Sound.

In its complete form the *Kabbalah* can be divided into two parts that correspond to two precise points of view: one includes the unfolding of the universal manifestation, and from this point of view is similar to the *darśana Sāmkhya* (this term, like that of *Sephirah*, means "numeration"); the second includes the metaphysical point of view of Ain Soph wherefore everything is seen as emptiness or as simple fleeting phenomenon.

Ain Soph may be compared to the *Turiya* of *Vedanta*, wherefore the *Kabbalah* may, along general lines, be said to be a synthesis of *Sāmkhya* and *Advaita Vedanta*, although the vision of this latter remains veiled in It.

'Ehjeh 'Asher 'Ehjeh means "I am What I am," "Being is Being," "I am Who I am," and is the Divine answer to Moses' question on Mount Sinai to know what His name might be.

This utterance may be compared also to the upanishadic *mantra*: "I am That," or "I am *Brahman* (*Aham brahmāsmi*)."

Raphael's aphorisms aim at making a simple contribution toward kabbalistic realization and, above all, they are meant for those who, wishing to emerge from the strictly magical viewpoint (in its various aspects) from which the *Kabbalah* is usually considered, seek to reach initiatory realization, which is the ultimate goal of the kabbalistic tradition.

————*Edizioni Āśram Vidyā*

The Sephirothic Tree

1. The sephirothic tree is a *mandala*, a symbol in which the innumerable expressive possibilities of the micro-macro-cosm are summarized.

Its proper interpretation reveals the meaning of the world of names and forms, and gives an understanding of gross and subtle energies, and of the possibilities of grasping them.

It may be "meditated" at the metaphysical, ontological, theurgical or psychological level.

Being a complete *mandala,* it is a symbol of noetic reality.

2. A symbol represents the reality that lies behind outer representations; in other words, behind every phenomenon, every appearance (*maya*) or form we find a universal creating principle, although invisible and sensorially intangible. Thus, the transcendent reality may manifest itself in an immanent manner by means of a symbol. From this point of view, the formal world itself is the symbol of the metaphysical reality. The symbol does not identify itself with the principle it expresses; therefore, in order to grasp the principle, one must avail of intuition.

3. The mistake that is normally made by the empirical mind (*manas*) is that of dwelling exclusively upon the symbol and, even more, attributing a conception and a representative connotation to it.

The mind interprets mere empty shells in a conceptual way because it cannot understand the principles that they manifest.

The empirical imaginative mind estranges us from the reality that the symbol proposes; it causes us to degrade and materialize the symbol itself to such a degree as to confine life to the world of shadows and appearances.

4. The Tree, which represents the basis of the *Kabbalah*, is a Pathway to realization. By meditating on and contemplating it continuously, one may realize the world of principles, its vital expression, the pathway of descent (solidification) and that of re-ascent (solution).

To consider the Tree a simple magical handbook suitable for prestidigitators means debasing It and emptying It of Its true contents. One must also recognize the fact that many disciples and scholars of the Tree fail to go beyond the material and psychical aspects and that their attention is centered exclusively upon the sephirah Yesod; that is, the sphere of sexual polarity, emptied of the intrinsic reality which, as a symbol, it reveals.

5. One must consider two aspects of the Tree—the involutionary and the evolutionary. However, it might be a good idea to eliminate these terms from an initiatory context, saying instead: falling and re-ascending, dreaming and awakening, the downward and the upward journey, the outward and the inward bound movement.

If we are to consider the Tree under its realizative aspect, it must be proposed from the point of view of its re-ascending or awakening function because initiation represents an expansion of consciousness that concerns universal and principial, or causal, factors.

Thus, if we wish to speak of initiation—and not of mere sexual or psychological magic—we must agree that the task of the disciple who approaches the Tree without ambiguity is that of "awakening" to the consciousness of Tiphereth first and then finally to that of Kether.

We must not forget that Adam is a fallen and stunned God, and that his task is to recover his primeval condition. From this stems the conception of "Awakening."

6. "Ten (excluding the Ineffable Ain) and not nine, ten and not eleven; understand and you will know," says

the Sepher Yezirah, "exert your intuition upon them, seek, discriminate, take note and set things back in their proper places, and place the Creator upon His throne."

"Ten sephiroth, except the Ineffable; their aspect is like that of dazzling flames, their fulfillment is to be found in the infinite. Through them the Word of God is revealed: by ceaselessly externalizing and internalizing themselves like whirlwinds of fire they fulfill the divine Word bowing before the throne of the Eternal.

"Ten sephiroth, save the Ineffable; their end is joined with their beginning like the flame with the burning coal; only the Lord is above them and has no second.

"What other number can you utter before the number One?"[1]

7. "It seems," writes Fabre d'Olivet (*The Hebraic Tongue Restored*), "according to the most prestigious Rabbis, that Moses himself, foreseeing the fate that his book might meet and the false interpretations it might undergo in time, took recourse to a spoken law which he transmitted orally to a number of trustworthy disciples, and that he gave them the task of transmitting it in the secrecy of the sanctuary to other men who in turn would transmit it from age to age so as to have it come down to remote posterity. This oral law... is called *Kabbalah*, from the Hebrew word which means 'what has been received,' 'what is passed from hand to hand.'[2]

---

[1] *Sepher Yezirah:* I, 3; I, 5, 6. Translation by Raphael.

[2] This translation was made from *La Langue Hébraïque Restituée* (*The Hebraic Tongue Restored*), p xxix. (Renens, Suisse: Editions L'age d'homme, 1975). *The Hebraic Tongue Restored*, by Fabre d'Olivet, was reissued by Samuel Weiser in 1991. This is a reprint of the 1921 English language edition and is a translation from the original published in 1815 in France.

There are two written scripts that may be considered the basis of the *Kabbalah*: the Zohar (Book of Splendour) and the Sepher Yezirah (Numeration); they contain the Old Testament's esoteric teaching.

8. If the Tree includes *also* a theurgical aspect, this term must be taken to mean *theos* = God, *ergon* = work or activity. Theurgy is not meant for practical, material, immediate, utilitarian ends and things of this kind, but for the union with the Divine, for the deification and the immortality of human beings.

In space-time, the consciousness has become identified with the more physical and solid aspects of manifestation. It has become "metallized," constraining itself more and more within the confines of the material and psychic spheres.

The Western Esoteric Tradition has gradually lost impact and ground (although it never died—a tradition cannot die, though it may become veiled, or obscured, or it may withdraw) because the people to whom it was directed have forgotten the Principle, that is to say, the metaphysical sphere, from which all things draw their origin and nourishment.

A culture and a science that lose this point of view, or rather, that stray from the metaphysical Principle cannot but perish because they have no basis upon which to rest.

All the traditional sciences have become degraded because their scholars have not taken into account the transcendent or metaphysical Principle. When knowledge is not based upon the Principle, it becomes mere technicality (whether scientific or magical) and a set of facts, concepts and words.

9. Although the divine expressions (intelligences) are indefinite, nonetheless the Tree divides them into ten

groups, because this number represents perfection. These divine expressions are called *sephiroth* (in the plural form) and *sephirah* (in the singular). The term means number or numeration.

The sephiroth are, therefore, the keys that open the doors to divine knowledge and to the *practical utilization* of such knowledge. They are hierarchical powers that operate in both the intra-individual and the universal sphere. It is important, therefore, to consider the number, the idea-intelligence and the name. We shall return to these concepts later.

10. In *Isaiah* (11:2) we read: "Above Him will rest the spirit of the Lord, the spirit of wisdom [Chokmah], of intelligence [Binah], the spirit of counsel [Chesed] and of strength [Geburah], the spirit of science and of pity [Tiphereth]...." And in *Chronicles* (or *Paralipomeni*) (I:29:11): "Yours, oh Lord, is magnificence [Chesed], power [Geburah], beauty [Tiphereth], victory [Nezach], glory [Hod]; because all the things that are in heaven and on earth are yours [Yesod = basis of everything]; yours, oh Lord, is the kingdom [Malkuth] and you are above all kings [Kether]."

"God, with Wisdom [Chokmah] created the earth, with Intelligence [Binah] he formed the skies. Due to his Science [Da'ath] the founts spring forth and the clouds yield dew" (*Proverbs*: 3:19, 20).

11. The sephiroth are the archetypes, the essential determinations, the prime causes, the principles of all manifest things. They are not distinct, opposite, individual entities; they represent various aspects of the One Reality (Kether).

They are simple modifications of the divine mind, they are ciphers of the sole power that is the One (Kether).

The Tree represents the unity of manifest and non-manifest life.

To separate one sephirah from all the others, giving it absolute value, means misinterpreting, altering and falsifying the sephirothic *mandala* and therefore the reality which it contains in synthesis.

12. A sephirah is an idea, a power-substance, an energy, a strength, depending upon the point from which one may wish to observe it.

In the field of science, one speaks of the force of gravity, of electronic energy, of the power of light, of the law of inertia. In other words, the universe is governed by forces, laws, and principles; therefore the sephirothic *mandala* represents power-forces or intelligences, the laws and the principles.

A law concerns the behavior of a power-force, of an intelligence. When one understands the sephiroth powers, one also understands the subtle laws that lie behind the gross world of names and forms which, in turn, represent the complexity of the elements of nature.

13. These intelligence-powers are called: Ain Soph Aur (the Infinite, the Metaphysical One, Non-Being as pure and unqualified Being, the Absolute, the One-without-a-second), Kether, Chokmah, Binah, Chesed or Gedulah; Geburah, Din (justice) or Pachad (fear); Tiphereth, Nezach, Hod, Yesod, Malkuth. There is also a veiled sephirah called Da'ath.

The *forms* or symbolic images normally attributed to the sephiroth are :

> *Ain Soph*: What is beyond names and forms. Ain = nothing. The Absolute cannot be intended except in terms of "not this, not this"

Kether: A King's face seen from the side

Chokmah: The face of a bearded man

Binah: An imposingly beautiful woman

Chesed: A crowned King sitting upon his throne

Geburah: A warrior King in his war chariot

Tiphereth: A beautiful regal figure. An innocent child
             or a glorious man on a cross

Nezach: A splendid nude Venus

Hod: A hermaphrodite

Yesod: An imposing naked man

Malkuth: A woman on a throne

14. As we said above, the sephiroth may be considered from various points of view.

From a philosophical point of view, the sephiroth are ideas, archetypes, universal principles that are beyond form and even beyond name. From a theological point of view, they represent the various divinities or the angelical hierarchies of Kether, as the creating God, and may be classified as follows:

1. *Kether:*   Chajoth or Seraphs

2. *Chokmah:*   Ophanim or Cherubs

3. *Binah:*   Aralim or Thrones

4. *Chesed:*   Haschemalim or Dominations

5. *Geburah:*   Seraphim or Virtues

6. *Tiphereth:*	Malachim or Powers
7. *Nezach:*	Elohim or Principates
8. *Hod:*	Ben Elohim or Archangels
9. *Yesod:*	Cherubim or Angels
10. *Malkuth:*	Ischim or Souls

From a universal psychological point of view, they represent the energetic qualities, vital psychic expressions. From the formal physical point of view, they represent interacting "substances"; thus Binah is the primordial elementary substance from which all gross, superphysical, subtle and noumenal bodies are made. Malkuth is, instead, the gross substance from which the various physical-material body-elements are made. The sephiroth, therefore, constitute *substances* at various degrees of condensation, vibration, and movement.

As we can see, the Tree may be studied from a physical, psychological, theurgical, philosophical—and if we consider Ain Soph—from a metaphysical point of view, too.

When referred to the Ways or Pathways, one finds correspondences with the metaphysical, philosophical, theurgical, and magical-occult pathways.

The sphere of Ain Soph regards pure metaphysics. Thus the Tree, in its wholeness, embraces the totality of knowledge. Each sphere includes the one below it; therefore the metaphysical vision includes the totality of the cognitive points of view. Each sphere reveals certain powers and faculties that are peculiar to the sephiroth in question.

15. When certain sephiroth—see Nezach, Hod or Yesod—become separated from the Principle on which they depend and from which they derive their *raison d'être*, their own expressive movement becomes degenerated, depraved and altered, leading obviously to error, conflict and profound aberration. When, for example, the sephirah Yesod is not subjected to the Principle, we have a pathological sex-maniacal degeneration typical of those who interpret life in a unilateral, neurotic and obsessive manner.

There are several works of "sexual magic" which prospect the acquisition of powers or even union with the Absolute, proposing exclusively sexual activity, even orgies; the more the orgy is free of subconscious, binding and repressive contents, the more it reveals Kether, the One, the universal God and first cause. This might lead one to think that Kether—the God-Person, the Lord of the world and of all worlds—and his intelligences have a predilection for brothels that, among other things, belong to a certain individualized order. We have to set things straight. We do not wish to banalize certain normal existential activities or disown them or to denigrate them in a moralistic way. Nor do we wish, either, to deny the *polar* function that is to be found within the manifest, and in particular within our expression of life. To avoid all misunderstanding, we wish to add that, on the other hand, true metaphysical vision does not exclude anything—and includes everything—only it makes everything depend upon the Principle.

16. It is necessary, however, to emphasize the fact that for the tradition polarity is inherent in the individual; thus, Adam has Eve within him (for the East, the individual is the polar expression of *Purusha* and *Śakti* which

are placed spatially at the Center of the head and at the base of the spinal cord) and that the *scission* occurred due to the "fall."

That which is split (duality) must be united (unity) and unity is achieved when Eve is resolved in Adam or when *Śakti*, awakening, reunites with *Purusha*. The doctrine of Tantrism, the one submitted to the Principle, teaches us that a man and a woman may operate within the sphere of Yesod so that a powerful concentration of *prana* is determined within their auras, and by means of correct positions and appropriate techniques and visualizations, can awaken *Śakti*, uniting it with *Purusha* or *Shiva*. But this type of union (because it is of union that one may speak rather than of coupling with a view to enjoy pleasure) excludes all kinds of gratifying elements. Only whosoever shall assume the solar position and not the lunar one shall vanquish the great Goddess *Kundalini*.

17. However, sex, as it is normally thought of, is the symbol of a more profound and more universal reality. When the symbol loses its "soul," or the content that is innate to it, it remains but a shadow, the shell of itself, void of expressive vitality.

Tradition expresses itself by means of symbols— *mandala* and pure ideas—and when the key to these symbols has been lost, people avail themselves of amorphous skeletons, of representations invented by the restless and incomplete mind of unilateral individuality.

The sephirothic Tree is a *mandala* symbol and if one does not possess the key (or keys) to its proper understanding, one makes of the sephiroth a game subjected to vanity and individual weakness. And it is known that by placing the emphasis upon "certain things" (sex, the acquisition of psychic powers of all kinds, etc.), one certainly attracts many followers.

The line of least resistance is for the majority, and it must be remembered that many are called but few are chosen. The "narrow doorway" is not for all, not because there are privileged or predestined people, but because not everyone wishes to "die while living," not everyone wishes to "cease being" in order to Be.

States of Life

18. As we have seen, the sephiroth are particular expressions, although impersonal, of the Kether-Unity and, even though each sephirothic attribute has its own archetypical connotation or its own ontological *number*, its hierarchical grade, and its particular influence, their essence or noumenal life is identified with indivisible and unqualified Unity.

The sephiroth are simply shades of the one principle color. A sephirah in itself and by itself can have neither existence nor influence; those who realize Kether synthesize sephirothic totality, like whoever realizes the Tiphereth consciousness synthesizes the lower set of four (Nezach, Hod, Yesod, Malkuth).

The sephirothic whole is not composed of the various sephiroth; it is not quantity that forms unity. The sephirothic whole is unity, itself, in its own specific expression. The "numerations" are simply spatial "points," and these points in turn are polarizations of the point without dimension.

If one forgets all this, one is bound to consider absolute a mere particular (with all the consequences of the case) which is an aberration of the empirical mind that is unable to grasp totality-unity-synthesis.

19. According to the *Kabbalah*, manifestation is divided into four states or existential worlds which we shall now compare with the doctrine of *Vedanta*:

Kabbalah	Vedanta
Aziluth	Turīya, nirguna Brahman
Briah	Iśvara
Yezirah	Hiraṇyagarbha
Assiah	Virāt

Aziluth is the sphere and the "root" of All; it is the Absolute and the substratum of formal and non-formal manifestation. A certain manifestation represents one of the infinite possible expressions of Aziluth. It is equivalent to the Ain Soph (the root of the Tree).

Briah is the principle creative sphere, it is the cause of manifestation, it is the first determination of Aziluth on the non-formal plane. Yezirah is the formative, animating sphere of subtle, archetypical manifestation; it represents the *anima mundi*, the universal plastic mediator. Assiah is the corporeal sphere of actualization, the sphere of the prototype and of objectification.

All the sephiroth operate within these spheres; they are, in fact, their creating, animating and molding powers. A plane of life is the actualization of sephirothic energy. There are sephiroth which animate certain planes or spheres and sephiroth that give life to other levels. Therefore sephirothic unity is to be found in the harmonic decade that causes indefinite vital effects; every effect or prototype is connected to its sephirothic archetype-principle and through this very archetype to the principial One or *'Ehjeh* (I am).

From the point of view of the physical sciences, the sephiroth that operate in the three worlds represent the vital *elements* of gross nature, the *energies* that move these elements, the *laws* ruling these energies, the sole *principle* upon which all is based.

20. Briah is animated by the Kether-Chokmah-Binah triad; Yezirah by the Chesed-Geburah-Tiphereth one; and Assiah by the Nezach-Hod-Yesod triad.

Malkuth may be considered as being the sephirah of simple "precipitation." It is the world of effect, of precipitates, of automatic actions; it is not the world of causes or of principles.

Aziluth, as cause of all causes, is therefore outside of principle and causal determination.

21. Going on to the microcosm, the *Kabbalah* considers the human being as a triune unit, and that is: *Neshamah* = spirit, *Ruah* = soul, *Nephesh* = body. When we make the appropriate connections we obtain:

AZILUTH

Macrocosm	Sephiroth	Microcosm
Briah	1st Sephirothic Triad	Neshamah
Yezirah	2nd Sephirothic Triad	Ruah
Assiah	3rd Sephirothic Triad	Nephesh

If we wish to attune ourselves with the sephirothic world of Assiah (Nezach-Hod-Yesod-Malkuth) we must simply assume as our *support* the sensorial-physical body. If the tonal accord must be achieved with the world of Yezirah (Chesed-Geburah-Tiphereth) one must avail of the support of Ruah—that is, of one's own Soul or of the body of glory which is in us. If, finally, we wish to attune ourselves to the world of Briah (Kether-Chokmah-Binah), we need the support of Neshamah—our own spiritual Essence.

22. If one desires to "walk" with Chokmah or Chesed, one must leave one's "shoes" at home. In His presence, one must bare oneself completely.

If we think that we can enter the sphere of the noumenal fire bringing with us our body of cells—perhaps even with its faults and particular desires—we are mistaken. We who think that we can realize the universal mind while remaining within our own particular and individualized mind enter into irreducible contradictions.

If we think we can realize unity while remaining attached to multiplicity, we are fooling ourselves.

If one keeps in mind what has been said here, one can understand why many followers of the *Kabbalah* operate within the sphere of Nezach-Hod and, above all, within that of Yesod, divorced from their superior principles.

23. The three sephirothic triads can be related to four speculative aspects—the metaphysical, the ontological, the psychological and the physiological.

1st TRIAD

Kether	Principial ontological sphere
Chokmah	Knowledge of identity
Binah	*Mens informalis* (unitary principle)

2nd TRIAD

Chesed	Archetypical universal sphere
Geburah	Intuitive knowledge
Tiphereth	(Archetypes)

3rd TRIAD

Nezach	The psychological and psychic sphere
Hod	Empirical-sensorial cognition
Yesod	(Plastic mediator)
Malkuth	The physical-corporeal sphere The five perceptive organs

Sephirothic Columns and Triads

24. The Tree appears in the following symbolical configuration:

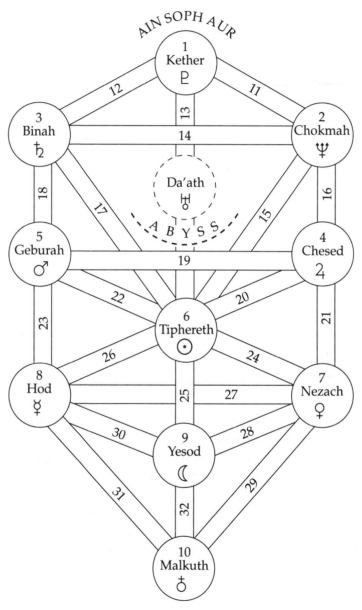

25. First of all we have to emphasize a fact: the Tree is composed of three columns, three pillars which represent the "skeleton" and which, for convenience sake, we shall call A, B and C in our illustration.

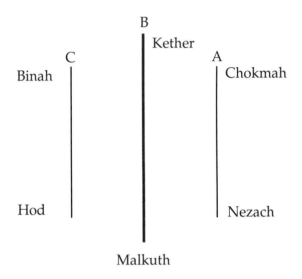

From the point of view of physics, A represents energy and power; C represents the element of nature, and B is the law. From the psychological point of view, the A column stands for conservation, clemency, mercy, benignity. The C column stands for rigor and creative activity. B regards synthesis, consciousness, balance. A and C are functions, faculties, powers that carry out activities. B, on the other hand, is awareness, the assimilation of polar action; it is the most subjective way, the furnace where the polar directions are amalgamated, fused, and reconciled. One speaks of polarity because A and C do not represent absolute duality, but a simple polarity (A = positive, C = negative) caused by B (Kether). In Kether—the God-Person—all sephirothic polarities are resolved, and the consciousness which finds itself along the line of the middle course, operates in terms of synthesis. One might say that polarity operates in an equilibrated manner when it is subject to the action of the central column, that is, of the just law.

In terms of *yoga* one has:

A = *pingala*: masculine, sun, positive

C = *ida*: feminine, moon, negative

B = *sushumna:* where the two currents or the *nadis, pingala* and *ida* are resolved

Other correlations are :

A = energy, *rajas*, air

C = form, *tamas*, water

B = life-consciousness, *sattva*, fire

The three pillars have a precise correspondence with the caduceus of Hermes. What is said of the Tree may also be said of the caduceus.

26. The left pillar represents the aspect of movement-action, the right-hand one the aspect of stimulus and propulsion. Binah is the night moving toward the dawn, Geburah is the dawn and Hod is the day. Binah, Geburah and Hod give form to the propulsive and undifferentiated energy of Chokmah, Chesed, and Nezach.

The left-hand pillar may be represented also as follows:

Binah	*Geburah*	*Hod*
Point	Line	Plane
Life	Quality	Form
Substance	Intellect	Mind
Root of motion	Motion	Appearance
	Subject	Object

From a qualitative point of view the right-hand pillar stands for:

Chokmah	= Will
Chesed	= Love
Nezach	= Activity

The Will is determined as a stimulus to form, as a power-sound that sets the "primordial waters" (Binah) in motion. Love appears as a proper polar relationship commensurate with life and universal justice. Love is proper tonal accord (Geburah). Activity is determined as intelligent creativity (Hod).

The pillar at the center represents the synthesis of the polar aspect, the assimilation of the formal-qualitative faculties by our consciousness, the axis of the world, the universal center, the Tree of Life. The left-hand and right-hand ones represent the Tree of Knowledge of "evil" and of "good," the way of rigor and of clemency, the way of the "powers."

As already said, when these powers are not subjected to the direction of the principle, we have "egoic magic," or power at the service of the empirical ego.

27. The sephirothic complex is divided into a further three triads:

Kether—Chokmah—Binah   = Life aspect
Chesed—Geburah—Tiphereth = Quality aspect
Nezach—Hod—Yesod   = Appearance,
                                                    aspect, form.

Malkuth, the tenth sephirah, represents the plane of precipitations, objectivity, and appearance; it is, as we have already seen, a simple effect.

Thus, on the opposite side, there is Ain Soph, which is the strictly metaphysical, unqualified, non-manifest principle. On the one hand it is the most dense objectivity and materiality, on the other, it is the most rarefied subjectivity and essence—alpha and omega.

The first triangle is non-formal and non-manifest, although principle or causal. The second is the subtle universal life-giver; the third is of the individualized psychical order. Thus we have the point, the line, and the plane. A triad is an operative unit upon a specific existential plane.

28. Every triad is formed by a polar aspect and by a point of synthesis, harmony, and of objective expression; wherefore, for example, one may obtain this type of triangulation:

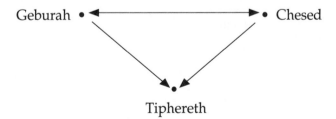

When there is an exchange of energy between Chesed and Geburah, Tiphereth is illuminated, revealing the potentialities of the positive and negative aspects of the two sephiroth. Therefore, in our case, Tiphereth is the expressive vehicle of the Chesed-Geburah polar combination.

29. We have said that the sephirothic triads operate upon certain existential levels, wherefore it is necessary to be very careful, when following the pathway of *total* awakening, not to get lost along the way. One must distinguish that which is gross-material, that which is subtle-energetic, that which is essentially principle and, finally, what is exclusively of the metaphysical order.

In order to have a precise idea of the Way of Return, it seems appropriate to propose an explicative table of the triads, proceeding from the bottom toward the top and leaving out Malkuth.

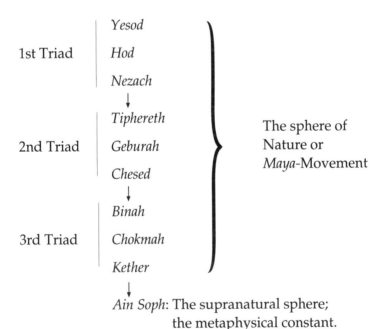

	Yesod	
1st Triad	*Hod*	
	Nezach	
	↓	
	Tiphereth	The sphere of
2nd Triad	*Geburah*	Nature or
	Chesed	*Maya*-Movement
	↓	
	Binah	
3rd Triad	*Chokmah*	
	Kether	

↓
Ain Soph: The supranatural sphere;
the metaphysical constant.

The metaphysical sphere is that of Ain Soph, and it is toward this that the disciple who follows *The Pathway of Fire* must tend.

Although some triads may express exceptional and universal qualities, nonetheless they are operating in the dominion of the natural, of the objective, of duality (subject-object), of becoming and, therefore, of time-space-causality.

The middle course is "The Pathway of Fire" which from Malkuth leads to Tiphereth, to Da'ath, to Kether, and finally, to Non-Being as Absolute-Constant.

The Pathway of Fire

30. We have spoken of the "Pathway of Fire" with reference to the *Kabbalah*, to *Advaita Vedanta* and to *Asparsa Yoga* and, although our readers have already understood its meaning, we feel it is nonetheless important to clarify its significance very thoroughly.

The "Pathway of Fire" has, obviously, nothing to do with the element of fire proper; it indicates the "Way" (*sadhana*) along which to travel in order to realize one's own essence. Even in *yoga* terms, one may say that the fire *Kundalini*, which resides at the base of the spinal cord, must join with the fire of *Shiva* which is at the top of the head. It is, therefore, an experimental, operative, realizative way.

We might also use the expression "The Pathway of Sound" (*shabda marga*) because sound, too, is subject to manifestation and the disciple realizes himself or herself as Sound, and finally as non-sound essence. *Om* is the primordial sound, it is the vibrating dart; even light is primordial fire. Thus, one may speak of luminous sound and of resounding light or fire. In Sanskrit "sound" is called *svara* and "light" *svar*; sound and light are thus united by their essential phonetic affinity. On the basis of this identity between light and sound, in the *Rig Veda* the singer is called the *svabhānavah*, that is, "he who is self-luminous."

According to the *Kabbalah* the light-verb emerged from the depths of darkness. Therefore the "Pathway of Fire" is the *way* that every disciple must travel along whatever branch of the tradition he or she chooses. This is the "Way of Return." As a result, it is not either a particular or individual teaching, nor again, a collateral way with respect to the sole and only main road. In truth such an expression sprang up innocently yet appropriately.

The author of these notes, having received the *Asparsa* and *Advaita Vedanta* teaching, was told, at a certain point of his *sadhana*, to light the fire, to burn himself in the fire and to dissolve himself in fire. This "way" has also a bearing on the God Agni, considered in the *Veda* as the Lord of the triple world. But Agni also represents the flame of aspiration toward the most High, which in the end fills the heart with the devouring fire of Pure Awareness. (It is obvious that certain suggestions can have a meaning only for whom they are given.) Later, studying some of the other branches of the tradition, he realized that, after all, each disciple, to whatever branch he or she belongs, follows his or her own "Pathway of Fire."

Yesod

31. It is now necessary to examine each sephirah again, beginning from the very bottom.

Yesod (= base) is the foundation of and the substance from which all things are made at an objective level. It expresses the "Lower Waters," while the symbol of the "Upper Waters" is Binah. Between Yesod and Binah there exist, therefore, precise correspondences; on the one hand Binah (primordial substance, equivalent to *Prakṛti* in *Vedanta*, the universal Mother-nature), stimulated by Chokmah-Kether, is the material cause of manifestation; on the other hand, Yesod (lower lunar nature-substance, more "material" and more gross) brings into objective manifestation (Malkuth) those imaginative impressions received from Hod-Nezach. In the human-microcosm, the reproductive organs correspond to Yesod. This fact illuminates the function of Yesod, just as at the highest level it illuminated the condition of Binah, if one considers it as being the universal Mother. In *yoga*, Yesod corresponds to *prana* (the superphysical element) and it is in the body-sheath *pranamaya* that the *chakra svādhiṣṭhāna*, the creator-center of the generating seed, exists.

Yesod is the quintessence of matter after the solid, liquid, gaseous, aeriform and, after the earth, water, air and fire elements. Therefore, it is substance which goes beyond the sensorial-material plane because it is a superphysical element. Every thing-event of the dense physical dimension originates in Yesod; every correction, transformation or transmutation which is thought of at the physical level must be prepared in Yesod.

Thus, every transformation which must be carried out in the cellular constitution of a human being must first occur in the gene which is the archetype-code of the physical cell. Yesod is pre-material physical substance in which the archetypes produced by Hod converge and are made concrete and then later precipitated as prototypes in Malkuth. The true "operations" must be prepared in Yesod, not in Malkuth. The Yesod substance is plastic, mobile, fluid, and sensitive to every kind of stimulus. As is well known, the electron is sensitive to the simple presence of an observer to such a degree that Heisenberg[3] was urged to formulate his theory of indetermination. But Yesod is sensitive above all to Hod which represents the mind, another even more pliable, more subtle, more powerful and penetrating substance.

With reference to sexual polarity, one must say that Yesod, being by nature the sphere that causes all objectivity, represents propulsion toward polar union with a view to generating and procreating. All sexual movements and impulses occur upon this level and avail of the corresponding physical organs for fulfillment and precipitation. Hyperstimulation in this sphere may lead to conflict and degeneration, and, as a result, it is only by turning one's attention toward that sphere, and not toward the physical sphere, that one can solve these problems.

It is not upon the dense plane that one must operate to solve certain organic disharmonies—in this precise case the sexual ones—but upon the plane of Yesod, as the second cause of disharmony and degeneration, and even more upon that of Hod-Nezach as the prime cause.

---

[3] Werner Karl Heisenberg (Wurzburg 1901-Munich 1976) is a German physicist who received the Nobel prize in 1932 for his work on atoms and the mechanics of quanta. His main works are *Physics and Philosophy* (New York: Harper Torchbooks, 1958); *Physics and Beyond* (New York: Harper & Row, 1971); (Lipsia: *Die physikalischen prinzipien der quantentheorie*, 1930); and for more information see also *The Tao of Physics* by F. Capra.

In conformity to the propelling power of Hod, the Yesod substance may crystallize an event-thing for such a long time that it becomes subject to the law of inertia. This gives rise to what is generally known as a subconscious content of the instinctive organic, material order.[4]

The human being, being a perfect copy of the macrocosm and synthesizing within the totality of life, possesses window-centers which open up upon the various existential planes. Generally these window-centers are closed (only the one on the dense physical plane is open), wherefore one is unable to either see or operate upon the various levels of life. One is often able to perceive them if gifted with a certain degree of "sensitivity."

There are two ways one can come into contact with the world of the powers:

A) By opening these window-centers and thus, in perfect awareness, *being* and operating upon the various planes.

B) By means of ritual, and in this case one performs theurgy. It is preferable to leave aside what is today commonly called magic.

---

[4] In other words, the event-thing, now being a subconscious content, continues proposing itself cyclically, as if it were an independent entity with a will of its own, and often in conflict with the will of the being who generated it; it is the "child that devours the father." For more information see the chapter on the origin of the subconscious in *Tat tvam asi—That thou art*, by Raphael (Rome: Edizioni Āśram Vidyā, 1977; English edition, Delhi, India: Motilal Banarsidass, 1992).

Hod

32. We stated earlier that Yesod is sensitive to the influence of Hod; rather, that its activity is determined by Hod, itself. Hod is the positive-active agent and Yesod is the negative-passive one; when they are joined together the precipitation of Malkuth takes place. In other words, when the idea meets the formative plastic substance, expression upon the objective plane is achieved; or, when a thought meets the vocal cords—which are nervous fibers—words or sounds expressing that thought are produced. An idea that does not become "flesh" represents a phenomenon of vain sterility and pure onanism that may prove harmful to the creator.

Hod is a mercurial substance even more vibrant and rarefied than that of Yesod, and what is called idea is its "son." An archetypal form projected upon Yesod not nourished by Hod is a body without a soul; one might say that it is a miscarriage. The archetypal images of Hod are energy vectors that mold the pranic-ethereal substance of Yesod. Hod does not act directly upon Malkuth, but upon Yesod. Hod is, therefore, creative thinking; in Hod the idea is contemplated, in Yesod the support and the suitable framework are created, in Malkuth the idea is expressed and materialized.

Thus one obtains a triple expression that represents the creative modality of the Gods and of human beings. This tripleness includes the spirit, the soul, and the body. The spirit is the nucleus-essence or the noumenon; it is the Entity, regardless of the nature, the dimension, or the level it may belong to; the soul is the formative *water*, the plastic mediator, the placenta that nourishes the nucleus to bring it to maturity; the body is the vehicle of the nucleus-entity's objective expression.

The true *demiurge* operates above all in the sphere of Hod; according to its contemplative power, Yesod automatically molds itself, causing the seed of contemplation to precipitate into Malkuth. A demiurge is not very interested in the raw material; the demiurge sees to it that the plastic mediator models itself appropriately on the basis of the propulsion force of the contemplative act alone.

33. Hod is essential noumenal substance, the principle (with regard to the individualized psychic triad) substance, but it receives the impulse of life from the sphere of Nezach. Hod becomes passive and negative toward Nezach, while toward Yesod, as we have seen, it is active and positive.

Nezach represents the original impulse to manifest love for life and living (its lower octave is represented by desire). It is the prime force of descent, of exteriorization, of precipitation. Without this vital impulse, Hod would not have the opportunity to organize as a nucleus, nor would Yesod as plastic mediator, nor, as a result would there be forms upon the physical-objective plane. Nezach is the force of nature that urges Hod *to formulate*. Its upper-middle octave is Chesed, and its universal supreme octave is Chokmah. Just as at a strictly objective level without desire one cannot obtain any formative effect, so, too, on this plane, without Nezach's willpower there is no impulse to think either; we mean "to think" and not to be thought; the majority are passive objects of thought disorder, that is why they do *not create*.

In Nezach the love-life-impulse proceeds toward the external, in Hod this impulse actualizes as noumenon, in Yesod it finds its animating food, and in Malkuth it becomes manifest and appears.

From this point of view we thus have a complete triad as well as a plane of precipitation.

Nezach   =   generating life—Venus

Hod   =   nucleus—emerging quality—Mercury

Yesod   =   molded archetype—Moon.

Nezach

34. Nezach means "victory," or "firmness," because it is the victorious and firm impulse which generates and determines upon the plane of Hod. One may also point out the following correspondences: Nezach is the inspirer, Hod the thinker, the composer, and Yesod the molder; Nezach intuits and wills, Hod geometrizes it and Yesod animates and precipitates it.

Without the propelling power of Nezach, Hod would remain sterile and, in turn, without the thinking impulse of Hod, Yesod remains still and latent. The mind taken in itself does not confer any power; if, however, it is electrified by the incisive and directional *potency* of Nezach, then it becomes a "tension field" ready to coagulate a *nucleus-entity*.

Nezach, Hod, Yesod, and Malkuth form the lower quaternary because they refer, as far as human beings are concerned, to individuality. Individuality is composed, in fact, by these sephiroth which, badly directed, create the urge to be selfish, to split and to differentiate. Thus, the life impulse of Nezach may be directed toward individualization. What is called the psychic world is composed of these three sephiroth (while Malkuth represents the physical element); it is the world of shadows. If one keeps in mind that the majority, in time-space, through the power of Hod, have created indefinite form-images which dwell in the subtle sphere, then one can understand why it is so difficult to perceive the true, the just and the beautiful.

By means of mental mercurial power, human beings created many psychic monsters which, as they were nourished more and more, superimposed themselves upon the true archetypes of the plane of Briah. One of these monsters is the empirical ego. This is a psychic compound with which the consciousness identifies. Ninety percent of magical ability, spiritism, pseudo intuitions, the power of mediums, the reception of sound and light, derive from image-forms belonging to the psychic order. They are so alive, so pulsating, and so concrete as to fool even the expert. The appearance of entities such as Christ, Buddha and others belongs to this intermediate psychic world. Many spiritual and occult texts come from *ghosts* belonging to the Hod-manasic (*manas* = mind) world superimposed upon the principle one. At times they are harmless inspirations, other times they are inspirations that create confusion and distort the truth. Sometimes they are evil and bring conflicts, deviations, and false truths concerning all the fields of human life to lead people down a "blind alley."

Antitraditional forces operate in this ghostly sphere created by irresponsibility and individual ignorance. The sphere of individuality, when it is not placed under the Power Tiphereth, works for the individual, for the particular, for self-assertion, or for the thirst of acquisition and enjoyment. Its action aims at compensating for a lack of wholeness that can be found, instead, in its transcendental state.

The human being is universal. If one seeks to circumscribe and limit oneself, one cannot but degenerate and perish. One is not only Nezach, Hod, Yesod and Malkuth, but also Tiphereth, Chesed and Geburah; in fact, the human being is much more. If one's direction is not upward, toward a completion of self, toward the awakening of the whole nature, one will find oneself travelling the road of *samsara*, of conflictual becoming and of compensation. Individuality *creates* all things in this world of ghosts *to compensate* for its impotence and restlessness. Those who operate magically only in this sphere contribute toward the creation of greater disorder and suffering.

Sexual magic (Yesod), ritualistic and imaginative magic (Hod), divorced from the directing principle of Tiphereth lead to a blind alley and to the world of Qelippoth, that is, a world of darkness, disharmony, and unbalance. One-sidedness, fanaticism, and selfishness are all unbalanced effects of universal harmonic reality.

Idea—Number—Name

35. Sephirah means "number" because it represents a certain degree or harmonic of the Kether-note; it also contains what the *Kabbalah* calls idea and name.

Universal unfolding and reabsorption are reproduced in a *numerical scheme* which reflects in its combinations the weave and architecture of the cosmic building and fixes its various stages.

The name is the Word of Power, the verb which the primordial Kether (the noumenal One, the fundamental sound) assumes upon that plane of existence. To pronounce the name of a particular sephirothic sphere means making it vibrate; it is like sounding the key of a piano. It means setting in motion the intelligence that governs that sphere. The existential totality of an entity is enclosed in a name and this is equivalent to luminous sound.

The idea is an intelligence, a power, a principle, a law acting in life, a universal center of personalized action. It is the name which has individualized itself—which has taken on a precise configuration.

Thus we have ten names which are the subsounds of the sole divine name-sound, and ten intelligences-powers, each with a lawgiving task to perform.

If the name is the cause of *movement* on a plane, idea-intelligence is its direction, its development, the principle that governs that plane.

With reference to the sephirothic triad which we discussed earlier, the name of Yesod's numeration is *Shaddai* (omnipotent), its idea-intelligence is the Archangel *Gabriel* (man of God) who is the head of the angelic host of the *Cherubim* (the strong). Every time one invokes these angelic hosts—which are particular vibrations producing certain effects—they answer.

Hod's sephirah-numeration has the name *Elohim Shabaoth* (God of the armies), while its idea-intelligence is

Michael (God-like) who is the leader of the angels *Ben Elohim* (Sons of God).

Nezach's sephirah-numeration has the name *Tetragrammaton Shabaoth* or *Adonai Shabaoth* (God of the Hosts), while its idea-intelligence is called *Haniel* (grace of God) who is the leader of the angels *Elohim* (Gods).

We should consider that in the *Haṁsa Upanishad*, which is a part of the *Yoga Upanishad*, the pathway of *Brahman* consists in the gradual recognition of ten sounds. At a certain point the *Upanishad* proposes: "We must transcend the first nine sounds and concentrate our attention upon the tenth which is that of thunder... he becomes *Brahman* at the tenth, realizing union of the soul with *Brahman*."[5] This *Upanishad*, as one can well see, is of the metaphysical order because it transcends the nine sounds that represent the world of *maya* or of nature. In kabbalistic terms one might say that one must transcend the nine sephiroth and resolve oneself in Kether. This is the Middle Pathway, the Pathway of Fire, the metaphysical way, that of initiation, and is for the one who has awakened to the awareness of being transcendent.

36. The name and form taken in themselves have no value. The name is nothing but a denomination of a force, an energy, an underlying reality. For example, one attributes the *name* "electron" to a certain energy-reality. The name separated from the named reality is pure nothing. Thus a form (an image, figure, face, or effigy) is a configuration, a representation, an aspect of reality. If, after all, the name and the form are simple *mental representations*, what they represent is, on the contrary, real.

---

[5]Haṁsa Upanishad, sutra 8, 11. Translation from the Sanskrit by Raphael.

To call a certain thing by its proper *name* means to *stimulate* it, render it active, responsive. To call an individual by his or her proper name means giving that individual the possibility to *answer*. From this point of view we may speak of *invocation*, which in turn causes *evocation*. These terms must be used in a very special sense, not in the sense that is normally attributed to them. Whoever understands the "law" of invocation and of evocation is capable of "dialoguing" with life.

It is obvious that if we apply this to the case of a single human being, to evoke a response we must only call that person's name—uttering the name verbally, using the voice, vocal sound—because this is the way in which the person can receive an invocation. This implies that every level, every sphere of life, or every existential plane expresses itself using its own language (sound) and its own form (color).

For example, if we wished to invoke Kether and started to simply call out this name, we could wait for years and cosmic cycles without ever receiving a response. What is meant here is something which genetically precedes any formulated name and all conceptual expressions based on logic. It is something primordial and above all concepts, therefore it bears no reference to intellectual understanding. The Ancient Egyptians called this undefinable aspect of the sound-name a "cry" of the God Toth. The *Haṁsa Upanishad* speaks of "thunder."

When we evoke within ourselves a name or a word, we can notice—if we feel sensitive toward that word— that, like the echo of a trumpet or of a bell, our being begins to vibrate, to respond until it is completely taken, exalted, at times even enraptured (*samadhi*).

More than of Word we should speak of resounding syllable; or, rather, of the vibrating monosyllable, because it evokes that "cry" or that primordial supraconceptual sound which gave origin to manifestation. The *Aitareya Upanishad* (I: 4) includes the primordial sound in the cosmic egg: "*(Purusha)* hatched it. And, having hatched it, his mouth opened wide like an egg. From his mouth came the *word*, from the word the *fire*, hence, sound and light, or, as we said above, luminous sound and resonant light-fire."

Sound is the vehicle of creation or destruction, and the name—that is, the particular resonant combination—represents its seal and its symbol. Thus, to pronounce that name means to cause all vital things that depend upon it to vibrate.

Let us recall the three data—name, idea, number, or sound, quality, number. The resonant combination depends on the scale number and the sound itself produces tones (ideas); name, idea, number (sound-vibration, quality, number) are a triune unity. One has, as a result, the sound that produces number and quality, or the number that produces sound and quality, etc.

Quality or tonal values are the subjective aspect, while number represents the objective datum.

The wealth of *sāman* is its musical tone (*svara*).[6]

Tao fills the whole universe. . . .
This essence may not be called up using noise, but using sounds.[7]

---

[6]*Bṛhadāraṇyaka Upanishad*: I: III: 25. Translation from the Sanskrit by Raphael.

[7]*Chuang-tzè*: XVI: 1. Translation by Raphael.

A sephirah-number constitutes an objective element of the idea-intelligence that presides over a particular existential plane. The name is the *harmonic* of the primordial note (Kether). To receive the quality-idea, it is necessary to re-educate one's consciential string, one's inner *sensitivity* (a condition that goes beyond the psychic sensitivity which is a simple animal *reaction*), so as to be able to attune oneself to the quality-sound-fire of a sephirah.

If one proceeds along the central *string* of the Tree (the Pathway of Fire) one has the possibility of perceiving and grasping the luminous resonant quality within (*to be* idea, to live sephirothic harmony), while if one operates upon the lateral *strings*, one obtains, above all, number-sound (rite), but then one must pay great attention because the operator's consciousness string, not being related to the qualitative power of the entity evoked, may break. Human beings always operate outside themselves, they are always the executors of ritual actions, be they scientists, magicians, philosophers, or musicians. Reality is within oneself and, in order to be able *to grasp and evaluate* life-reality, one must experience it, that is, *vibrate* it; one must *be*. The expressive quality of life may be vibrated and experienced by an appropriately trained *consciousness string*.

It is necessary to reflect on the fact that the *Kabbalah* is not a set of formulæ for playing cards, or a book for calling up the "dead," or a recipe-book of magic for prestidigitators, or a form of religious mysticism as is normally meant by this term.

The *Kabbalah* is a traditional science and metaphysical discipline; therefore, it acts within the great and the smaller mysteries, it is *apara* and *para vidyā*.

The science of invocation-evocation, as it is of a specific vibratory order, of a certain position of consciousness as it requires appropriate rhythm, cannot be taught to all. It implies adequate qualification because it is also the fruit of intuition. Thus, one must not put oneself "before" the law-force, but *be* that law-force, especially if one touches the world of formless principles.

The human being is a center of resonance capable of receiving and of transmitting the verb. The human being is a *vessel* that may be filled and pour forth; one does not require a material temple in order to act and *attract* the intelligences because one is oneself a temple, the living symbol by which the idea reveals itself.

37. Therefore, one must distinguish between *realizing* a power (until one achieves *unity* with it), and placing oneself upon the plane of magical and objective dualism.

Doubtless, the first method implies transfiguration, accord, and comprehension of oneself; it means revolutionizing one's own incompleteness and limitedness, it means transcending the formal; the second implies only empirical practice and training.

The majority prefer ceremonial magic of a formal order because they do not wish to transform themselves or work upon themselves, but simply want to gather crumbs of curiosity, crumbs of insignificant information concerning this or that, or work with energies to dominate the weak and ignorant, to use tricks that baffle the ingenuous.

The sephirothic Tree does not represent an operative means by which to win for oneself the sympathies of some sephirah or other, but the Path of Fire by which to be Gods, rather than human beings, a path to reveal Kether, and, for those who are prepared for it, to integrate with Ain Soph Aur.

38. The human being is a being to the image and likeness of Kether and one has in oneself the vibratory wholeness that exists in the entire cosmos. One's inten-

tion must be that of *striking* within oneself those chords capable of making one attune to the universal existential intelligences. In this way one universalizes oneself and becomes a co-participant in the existing whole.

When, for example, one *vibrates* love, one syntonizes with Tiphereth-Chesed. We insist upon the concept of *vibrating with* rather than just saying (by means of the vocal cords) the name of the sephirah or the intelligence.

If the universe is upheld by vibratory entities which express *qualities* and, therefore, influences, by evoking within ourselves those qualities we can relate to certain entities. If wishing to evoke the central Chesed-Geburah-Tiphereth triad, we vibrate within ourselves hatred and separateness, we run the risk of attracting the *influences* of Qelippoth, rather than those of the desired triad.

The kabbalistic universe is composed of ten musical strings that resound with certain qualities, which in turn emit specific influences. The individual, in totality, possesses these string-windows and if able to resound them he or she enters into contact with the universal symphony. The disciple who pursues *The Pathway of Fire*, or the operative or realizative way, must know how to find within the right notes capable of enabling him or her to belong to the universal confraternity of the harmony of the spheres.

Normally we express qualities that attune us to the unbalanced aspects of the sephiroth. The task of the Tree is to stimulate the consciousness to express accord, harmony and the unity of life, and enable those who are prepared to completely transcend the world of vital *qualities* (the pure metaphysical pathway). To implement all this, we must consider that the lower triad receives its *raison d'être* from the middle triad, and if we were to separate the two, we would transform individuality into an absolute entity, devoid of soul and spirit.

Thus, if we wish that Nezach, Hod and Yesod achieve harmony with universal life, that the microcosm be attuned to the macrocosm, then we must place the emphasis upon the Tiphereth note. This implies realizing not a downward but an upward way; this means raising the tones; it involves transcending ourselves as simple individuality or specific part and subjecting ourselves to the principle; that principle which is the effective center of being.

To have an idea of what this means we may take a look at the following set of triads :

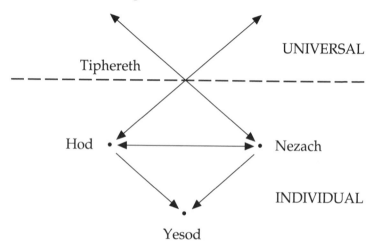

From this table we can deduce that:

A) The lower triad is the symbol of the upper one.

B) Yesod is the creative center of the lower triad and Tiphereth is the creative center of the upper triad.

C) Hod, Nezach and Yesod are the channels through which individualized consciousness can express itself. Tiphereth, with Geburah and Chesed, is the channel of universal consciousness.

D) The passage from the individual to the universal occurs following the destruction of the ego or egoic level. This implies undertaking initiation, real initiation, because all those that are usually given objectively are merely symbolic.

E) The individual operates through instinct (Yesod), feeling (Nezach) and imaginative mind (Hod); the universal operates through light-intuition (Tiphereth), love-harmony (Chesed) and willpower (Geburah).

The Pathway of Return

39. The path or way which leads from Yesod to Tiphereth is the 25th, called "Intelligence of Temptation" or "Pathway of the Trials."

The "Pathways of Wisdom" are the luminous roads along which one may arrive at the hidden Center. There are thirty-two of these.

40. The *chakras* corresponding to the sephiroth in question are shown below.

Chakra	Sephirah	Physical Organ
Svādhīṣthāna	*Yesod*	Generation
Viśuddha	*Hod*	Larynx
Maṇipūra	*Nezach*	Solar plexus
Anāhata	*Tiphereth*	Thymus/Heart

41. To implement the process of reorientation and solution of the energies one may follow three kinds of spiritual ascent which rest—according to the case—upon willpower, harmony-beauty and knowledge (the central triad).

It is obvious that such a process of death and rebirth must be guided by an expert kabbalist who has been initiated into Tiphereth and who, finding himself or herself consciously on the supraindividual plane, may as a result lead others into the universal.

There are people who know how to will, understand or feel the rhythm and the beauty everywhere.

By means of willpower one may achieve understanding and grasp harmony-beauty, or by means of harmony-beauty one may discover understanding and will-justice-equilibrium; and, again, through understanding one may discover harmony-beauty and universal willpower.

Understanding devoid of harmony-beauty, equilibrium, or universal justice remains unbalanced. In actual fact, one may say that one has not attained Tiphereth; or, rather, by evoking Chesed, instead of passing through Tiphereth it passed through Nezach and then through Hod, creating in this way an unbalanced passion (Qelippoth). Religious fanaticism, which sometimes becomes criminal, stems from this kind of unbalancing of the individuality that has been over-stimulated by a superior power. This is also true of will (Geburah) that passes directly through Hod and not through Tiphereth.

If one is not careful and well-guided in the evocation of the intelligence-powers, over-stimulation with a consequent scission of individuality may occur.

Universal *dharma*-will is well explained in the Bhagavad Gita. This will is, obviously, not of the individual, partial, sectarian kind; it is not even a type of willpower that can be associated with a particular realm of nature. All the kingdoms of nature express qualitative, universal archetypes and therefore the primordial archetype.

The lower quaternary group separated from the intermediate triad can develop and even refine the various senses, so that *manas*-Hod may increase utilitarian intelligence, certain defense mechanisms (and not only physical ones) as well as faculties for offense (even going as far as to invent very sophisticated means), but it can not develop that sense of universality, of all-inclusiveness, of vertical spirituality capable of carrying out synthesis and unity of consciousness.

What is normally called "progress" is a kind of monstrous ability and an unbalanced intelligence both of which operate for the preservation of the ego, meant as body and as psyche. This supposed progress, in actual fact, obscures that "sensitivity" which leads to synthesis, unity, and to the transcendent spirituality. Acquisitive and preserving intelligence that operates exclusively within the individual order does not allow the consciousness of "fallen" man to progress at all. So-called progress is nothing but a phenomenon of metallization, of solidification or terrestrialization, that is to say, a limitation of human awareness. The progress of an individual is determined insofar as one is able to fit into the context of universal harmony, to recognize oneself as an active element (or as a link in the cosmic chain of life), to discover that one is a brother among brethren, and not only within the ambit of the human life modality.

42. One thing must be taken into consideration: many believe that they are already integrated individuality, but this is not so—luckily. There are very few who will, think, feel and act.

The majority of individuals express certain "energies" and the center-consciousness automatically and impotently identifies with them. Thus, according to the energy of the moment—thought, emotion, instinct—they are compelled and conditioned. Their energy faculties are torn apart, separated and not coordinated by the center-consciousness. There are people who are compelled and conditioned by a certain line of thought, others by certain emotional-sentimental directions, without their knowing it. This disassociated wanting, thinking, or feeling enters into a relationship of "sympathy" with the collective unconscious causing ulterior reciprocal conditioning—certain interactions that urge people to greater degrees of automatism. When certain sephirothic Energies are evoked, the situation becomes even more complicated, because individualized energy currents are overstimulated and strengthened, but not integrated in the ego-consciousness. Thus certain tendencies and maniacal sexual obsessions with unilateral interpretations of reality are unleashed. One may end up with a conceptual, sentimental, or sexually-instinctive accentuation of reality. One may also, as often happens, be obsessed by a will for power or, to put it more appropriately, by a *desire* for power characterized by a need to gratify the ego-center. There are spiritualists and even initiated who have developed and strengthened the Hod-mind and have been dragged—despite themselves—onto the plane of criticism, opposition, and dogmatic individualism. People like these may even transform themselves into henchmen who take up the vindictive hatchet instead of the rod of imperturbability. They use concepts magically in order to strike rather than reveal truth innocently; and all this while employing words such as universality, understanding, vital unity, reason, identity, metaphysical reality. There are also adepts who speak in the name of love and brotherhood, but with such a degree of blindness as to be capable of awful revenge if someone dares to oppose them. The former kind are more dangerous because the magic powers of Hod have no limits, the *manas*-Hod may be capable of anything; it creates formidable alibis that few can resist; upon the plane of the word all are right and all are able to find valid justifications and defenses. Outrages, absolutisms, envy, acrimony, separativeness, revenge, crime and a thousand other things can all find a justification only because the magical power of the conceptual imagination is put to the service of the egoic monster.

Here we are undoubtedly within the realm of Qelippoth, obsession, and alteration of the proper Accord. If the strengthening occurs at the level of the ego (as a directional synthesis of the faculties), and not at the level of the single faculties or particular psychic power, the danger is even greater. It is so great, in fact, that we wish history, which has known several such cases, would produce increasingly less of them as time goes on.

43. Chesed, Geburah and Tiphereth, as we have seen, represent the central triad, the universal Soul, the intermediary between the objective and the integrally subjective. If one may compare deep night to the primordial or principle triad and day to the material triad, the idea of dawn may be connected with the central one.

The lower triad individualizes because it is selective, the central triad universalizes because it is synthetic; the former operates principally upon the plane of "dispersion," the latter upon that of cohesion and union.

These terms are simply symbols that express peculiar energies or intelligences. In the physical world, we have energies that express cohesion, fusion, or fission, and energies that express dispersion, disgregation, or scission; these forces are the effects of causes that originate from the central triad. As long as these forces are balanced there is life and harmony; when, due to certain circumstances, they become unbalanced, there is death and disharmony.

The Sun acts as a bipolar force of attraction and repulsion at the same time toward its planets. If this force were to become unbalanced, this would inevitably lead to the death of the planets because they would either be attracted and completely absorbed by the Sun, or thrust off, hurled away out into interstellar space. The same is true of the physical atom: if its cohesive-repulsive balance did not function harmoniously it would die.

Chesed-Geburah is a bipolar, cohesive-repulsive intelligence-energy and has its point of harmonic expression in Tiphereth. Now, if the individualized consciousness of the lower triad fails to respond to the harmonic rhythm of Tiphereth, it disintegrates and splits up until it is scattered in a chaotic manner. To make a correlation, it is the Tower of Babel. (At present on planet Earth, and on the human level, there are two political-social forces at work; the one is individual and selective, the other cohesive, communitary and collectivistic, but they are in opposition, they strive one against the other, besides being, both of them, exclusive and rigid. If one could find the point of union, which obviously transcends the materialistic conception of the one force and of the other, humanity might well be able to march toward a fruitful period of harmonic and stable interrelations. By meditating the sephirothic Tree in full depth we can also find explanations to specific human problems.)

If the lower triad wishes to operate harmonically, it must raise its eyes up to the sky and follow the way of Tao, the way of heavenly harmony, the way of beauty-order, the way of universal fire. The earthly Jerusalem must conform to the heavenly one.

The Initiated-in-Tiphereth live in this Jerusalem or in beauty-order, because they have made themselves subject to it having restored their cohesive-selective powers to the proper archetypical rhythm.

The Tiphereth-Consciousness revealed by the greatest *Avataras* has brought cohesive-selective energy onto the physical plane.

Jesus said that, besides universal love, he had also brought the sword. Samkara brought cohesive and unifying knowledge but also revolution; the same is true of Buddha; but their actions were in harmony with universal order, while in many of their followers there was more selective, individualized and, at times, oppressive energy (unbalanced Geburah).

44. It is advisable to remember that to evoke the sephiroth Chesed or Geburah without first harmonizing

one's own individualized energies means overstimulating certain flows of energy which operate within our psychophysical spatiality; this means heading, without realizing it, toward the realm of Qelippoth; it is in this way that we are enslaved by maniacal-sexual, passionate-sentimental or conceptual-representative expressive one-sidedness.

We wish to insist once more upon the fact that the immediate goal of the kabbalistic disciple is the evocation of the Tiphereth sephirah and of the Raphael intelligence which presides over that sephirah.

Tiphereth expresses beauty which is order, eurhythmics and sacrifice because it donates itself, offers itself, and concedes itself so the darkness may be illuminated. Tiphereth is dominated by the Sun and represents the first major initiation; with the eye of Tiphereth one sees universe-life in terms of harmony, of accord, of order and of understanding. It also represents the cosmic Christ-love, the master of life, the central heart, the reflected Sun of its upper pole, Kether. Tiphereth is the son of Kether upon a particular existential plane, just as the terrestrial Christ is the son of the heavenly Father.

45. As has been said elsewhere, there are many who instead of reaching Tiphereth love to amuse themselves by manipulating strictly individualized energies for profane, utilitarian and enslaving reasons; but one must also say that there are many who, having reached maturity, and having challenged the "powers" of certain inferior material spheres, know how to take flight toward the majestic peaks of wholeness and fullness.

46. Kether is the One in which all *is*, from which all proceeds and to which all returns. Da'ath is the first-born which operates upon non-formal levels; it is the universal mind (*Mahat*). Tiphereth is the second born, which oper-

ates upon formal levels. "Whoever sees Me, sees the Father." This is the awareness of Tiphereth. This sephirah is a ray of light from Kether offered to formal-objective beings who live in the darkness of individuality so that they may be able to find the way of beauty, justice, and goodness. Tiphereth is the universal Christ given as a gift to the sons of human beings so that they may become sons of God.

The salvation of conflictual, unilateral and passionate beings resides, therefore, in Tiphereth, because it is the central, mediating and unifying sephirah; it is the true heart of Kether, the heart which unites and fuses within itself the upper and the lower, the right-hand and the left-hand sides of the Tree. Tiphereth is considered as being the small face because it synthesizes the six sephiroth of the universal edifice.

Kether—Chokmah—Binah

47. The first sephirah is called the Crown (because it stands above all the others), the old man, the primordial or the smoothed point (when the *Setīma de-kol setīmīn*, mystery of mysteries, decided to reveal itself, it created first of all a sole point; initially the Infinite was completely unknown and did not give off any light before the manifestation of this point of fire), the white head or the long face. It contains all the other sephiroth and it revealed them in the following order: the masculine, active, or positive sephirah called Chokmah and its opposite, negative, passive, feminine pole called Binah. These two poles, also called *'Abbā* (father) and *'Immā* (mother) produced the unifying power called Da'ath (all-knowledge) which remained hidden, veiled, or esoteric because it is to be found upon the non-formal, principle plane. The triad (Chokmah-Binah-Da'ath) caused the polarity Chesed (masculine, positive, active) and Geburah or Din (feminine, negative, passive); in turn this polarity produced the unifying power of Tiphereth.

This unifying intelligence gave rise to masculine, positive, active Nezach and its opposite, feminine, negative, passive pole, Hod. This polarity produced the unifying power of Yesod which, in turn, precipitated Malkuth, also called *Shekinah*, upon the plane of objectivity.

48. The initial or principal triad—Kether, Chokmah and Binah—expresses the primordial diffusive aspect; it represents the seed of universal Life at the as yet non-manifest state.

It is the prime cause (while the central triad is the second cause of objective life), it is the noumenon of the manifest and non-manifest whole.

In Him (Kether) all is right hand, because the left is turned toward the infinite, Ain Soph.

Kether is also considered as the supreme crown, the central point of the circle, the ancient of the days, the Amen, the inscrutable height and the Aun. His name is *'Ehjeh* (= I am); and his idea-intelligence is called *Metatron*. He is the God-Person adored by mystics and by the religious in general. In reality, he is not a person in the everyday sense; humans anthropomorphize the very principles. Kether is existential essence, pure Being from which all springs; it is certainty of the unity of life, it surpasses all possible duality and fragmentation. In the eye of Kether what for us is multiplicity appears as undivided unity. Multiplicity is nothing but appearance, visual distortion unable to embrace the micro- and macrocosmic, individual and universal, formal and non-formal unity-synthesis.

Kether, seen from the point of view of the individual, is immanent and transcendent, inside and outside, but from its own standpoint it is neither the one nor the other because it transcends all dualism invented by Hod-Nezach. It is the crown which is set above the head because it includes all existence; It is above the Universal Man or Adam Kadmon, above the manifest Intelligences themselves—will, love, knowledge.

Whoever shall approach Kether shall approach the death of all formal and qualitative conditions, however much his essence may be "substantiated" with form and quality.

Kether is the central pillar of the arrow, of meekness or equilibrium and its experience, if we can speak of experience, it is that of union, or better still, of identity.

The true White Magician is he who, before every operation, becomes harmonized with the Kether-Metatron Power (and, obviously not only in words). The true kabbalistic magician is one who has laid down every burden and vessel to allow divine love-harmony to flow through one's "instrument of contact."

We have mentioned that the Kether experience is identity with the essence, which implies being beyond every evocation, beyond all energy, beyond the world of the intelligences, beyond theurgy and all that implies duality and gross or subtle form. The realization of Kether passes through the *via negationis* or, rather, through the solution of both the lower and intermediate triad.

49. Kether, the One, the primordial point is polarized in Chokmah and Binah, forming a triune Unity. The two points at the base of the triangle are, therefore, the polarization of the point at the apex.

The sephirah Chokmah represents supreme wisdom, the fruit-bearing ray of primordial light (father) which is the cause of the fertility of Binah (mother).

His name is *JeHoVaH*. His intelligence-idea is *Raziel*.

> I (Chokmah-Wisdom) love those who love me and whosoever seeks me will find me...
> God created me right from the beginning of his acts, even before his works...
>
> The abyss did not as yet exist: I was conceived when the fonts did not as yet gush forth...
> When he fixed the skies I was present,
> when he drew a circle
> upon the face of the abyss...
> ...whoever finds me finds life
> and obtains the favor of the Lord;
> he who loses me wounds himself; and he who hates me
> has chosen death.
>
> (*Proverbs*, VIII: 17, 22, 24, 27, 35)

The sephirah Binah represents the molding, creating primeval intelligence. Its name is *Jehovah Elohim*, its intelligence-idea is *Tzaphkiel*.

Polarity

50. It has been said that Chokmah represents the supreme father ('Abbā), the stimulator of the universe, and Binah the mother ('Immā; Marah = the great sea); one may express oneself in other terms and consider Chokmah as essence and Binah as substance, or Chokmah as a ray of white primordial light and Binah as the instrument through which the prism of colors appears. Binah is the great sea, the primordial waters, the receptive and life-giving darkness of the abyss. They may be compared also to *Purusha* and *Prakṛti* as in the *Sāṃkhya* or *Vishnu* and *Brahmā* of *Vedanta*.

On the level of human physiology, they represent the male spermatozoon and the female ovum; their encounter causes a third factor, which is the son of polar union. The son is the fruit of unitive bliss (*ananda* = love).

The intelligences, the universal forms belonging to every order and level are the daughters of 'Abbā-'Immā.

Binah, as the creating material cause of the world of names and forms is also destructive; in Binah forms are born and in Binah they grow and die; from this point of view its image is Severity (*Kali*); in fact it constitutes the beginning of the left-hand lateral pillar called the Pillar of Severity, while Chokmah is the beginning of the Pillar of Clemency-Benignity.

Make sure that you do not confuse these two terms (Severity-Benignity) with their ordinary psychological, moral, and individual connotations.

"Forms" are simply tools, instruments, or cellular compounds by means of which life circulates and qualities are revealed. Depending on the qualities and life, the forms change, undergo variations, and assume new expressions. For Chokmah-Binah, they are a prestidigitator's "trick," concrete movement, therefore *maya*, to say it in *Vedanta* terms.

What appears cannot but disappear, what is born cannot but die; thus, the Giver of formal life cannot but be the Giver of death; but apparition and disappearance are tricks of illusion—simple fleeting phenomena which may be considered as dramatic events only by a consciousness that conceives them as absolutely real.

As we can see by examining the symbol below, the progression of the various subpolarities occurs according to a specific order.

The study and understanding of these polarities (and of their points of synthesis) in all their various configurations—of which the sexual one is simply one and the lowest—afford the key to the many doors (fifty according to the *Kabbalah*) leading to the many pathways of wisdom, that is, to liberation.

It is hardly necessary to say that the two terms— primordial ovum and spermatozoon—represent a simple analogy and an exemplification of the ontological reality.

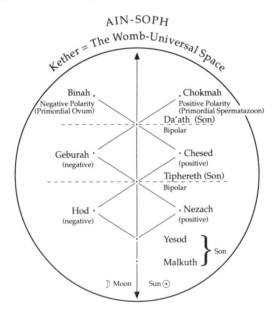

51. "The *Kabbalah* describes the process of the birth of the universe in other ways too, for example by recurring to the image of the *Pargod* or the cosmic curtain. The *Zohar* says that the 'Elder of elders' drew in front of Himself a curtain upon which an image of His kingdom appeared. . . . We may say that the more God lowers His curtain before Him the more He retreats into Himself. The curtain rises before Him like a darkness which identifies itself essentially with its cosmic receptivity in which His infinite light is interrupted or stopped, as it were, by a veil, wherefore it appears only a distant and weak reflection of Him, like the vain existence of all which is finite.

"God is hidden in all which is created, almost like the light in the innumerable sparkles of an enchanting mirage. The desert in which the mirage is created is the symbol of the cosmic emptiness, or the 'place of the world' in God's bosom, created by *Zimzum* (contraction of divine luminous fullness), while the elusive screen—upon which are projected the illusory forms that fool the passerby—is the symbol of the curtain or of the mirror of God, of his creative self-receptiveness, the *Shekinah*. Confronted with the 'One without a second,' the entire creation with its archetypes—in that they are not absorbed by the sole Reality but emanate the things created— assumes the illusory appearance of a 'second.' Therefore the *Kabbalah*, in order to define the nature of the creation, accompanies the ideas of *Zimzum* and *Pargod* with that of vanity—illusion—or *Habel* derived from *Eccles.* 1, 2: 'Vanity of vanities (*Habel habalim*)!... All is vanity (*habel*)!' And the *Zohar* comments: 'In this book King Solomon spoke of the seven vanities (*habalim*) upon which the world rests; they are the seven columns (the sephirothic columns of the Cosmic Edifice) which sustain the cosmos in its seven heavens (from which they are derived), *Vilon, Rakija, Shechakim, Sebul, Ma'on, Machon, Araboth* (as well as in their seven earthly effects or 'seven earths' and finally even their hellish darknesses or 'seven hells'). It is concerning these that Solomon exclaimed: 'Vanity of vanities!... All is vanity!' There are seven heavens or firmaments and others (deeper existential planes) that (they too are divided into seven) derive from these and remain united with them, so that we have seven (fundamental) vanities and others that derive from them (all of which taken together form the great illusion of the 'second'). In his wisdom, Solomon spoke of these illusions (as well as of their archetypes and causes, that is of the seven sephiroth of the cosmic edifice)."[8]

According to *Advaita Vedanta*: "Certainly *maya* has two powers: the projective one (*vikṣepa-śakti*) and the veiling one (*āvṛti-śakti*). From the subtle body to the gross one, all is created by the projective power."[9]

Pargod (curtain or cosmic veil) is equivalent to *āvṛti-śakti*, and *zimzum* (limitation, contraction, projective concentration) to *vikṣepa-śakti*.

The Tree or Cosmic Edifice, in its various dimensions and upon its various levels, seen by Ain Soph, is nothing but a simple projection or a weak reflection of the reality without a second.

The ten sephiroth represent ideal "modifications" of Kether and even Kether is only a reflection of Ain Soph.

---

[8] Leo Schaya, *L'uomo e l'Assoluto secondo la Qabbalah* (Milan, Italy: Rusconi, 1976), p. 84, 85.

[9] Dṛgdṛśyaviveka, sutra 13. Translation from the Sanskrit and commentary by Raphael, (Rome, Italy: Edizioni Āśram Vidyā, 1977); English edition: *Self and Non-Self* (London: Kegan Paul, Ltd., 1990).

If to the word reality we wish to give the meaning of infinite, uncaused, constant, absolute, outside of time-space-cause, then we can attribute it only to Ain Soph. Kether is a simple spatial-temporal "harmonic" of the infinite possibilities of Ain Soph. Kether is the Principle, the non-manifested Unmoved and the ten sephiroth are the movement; beyond motion and non-motion Ain Soph—the Absolute without a second, undifferentiated substratum from which objective reflections depart and radiate—exists.

If we find ourselves in the lower triad, Nezach-Hod-Yesod, we are in the shade and in the realm of essentially fleeting phenomenon; if we find ourselves within the central triad of Chesed-Geburah-Tiphereth, then we are in the world of ideas or archetypes; if we find ourselves in the upper triad, that of Kether-Chokmah-Binah, then we are in the principle, causal, generating world; and if, finally, we find ourselves in Ain Soph we are beyond shadows, ideas and principle; therefore, we are in the infinite, in the one and only reality, wherefore we have reached the deepest levels of *Pax profunda*, bliss without object; we are in the sweetness of the unconditioned and boundless.

The "Pathway of Fire" winds its way along the central pillar; it touches Malkuth, Yesod, Tiphereth, Da'ath, Kether, and, in the end, Ain Soph. There are five centers that we must burn within our own psychic space, five skeletons that we must reduce to ashes.

52. We said before that the pathway which from Yesod leads to Tiphereth is the twenty-fifth, that of temptation or trials. This implies that, on our descent, the individualized world represents a strong temptation and a trial for the soul which sets out along this path.

Along the ascending line, to find oneself again in Tiphereth, one must:

A) Resolve the crystallizations created by Hod; these are living form-images that dwell within individual psychic space and make life subject to the laws of inertia.

B) Stop the descending motion of energies, which implies making oneself the neutral center of the "ebb and tide" of energy.

C) Re-orient psychic movement in an upward direction, thus resolving the horizontal way of the individual; in other words, one must make a U-turn; this involves moving from an exteriorized to an interiorized state.

This ascesis which demands *solution, fixation* and *re-orientation* cannot be described because it belongs to the particular subject who undertakes the ascesis. Each disciple has his or her state of consciousness, *karma*, kind of energy, etc., and ascent must be considered in connection with these data.

In any case it is possible to offer those who are ready some brief explanations.

53. There is no *form* or *quality* that does not tend toward its own extinction, toward its own death, its own annulment.

Great efforts are made to perpetuate the world of form and the qualities it expresses with a great waste of energy; and yet its end—despite all efforts to the contrary—is transformation (beyond form) and transquality (unqualification).

In terms of physics, being is *form* (body-volume); in psychology it is *quality* (psyche); in theology and philosophy it is *consciousness-life* (principle); in metaphysical terms it is *one-without-a-second*, absolute constant, un-qualified and uncaused infinite. Thus we have:

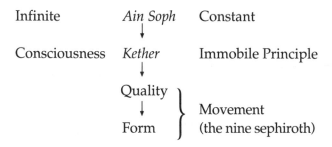

We can *feel* the reactions of the form, we can *feel* the qualities apart from the form and we can *feel ourselves* as being peaceful life interwoven with silence—life which rests in itself and for itself. When we have reached the great silence, the consciousness, having resolved all motion, is attracted by Ain Soph.

54. "One" is the consciousness, "two" is the quality, "three" is the form; the three are not separated but represent different modes of vital expression of the undivided unity.

"One" is silence (Kether), "two" is movement (Chesed-Geburah-Tiphereth), "three" is prison (Nezach-Hod-Yesod).

The "Pathway of Fire" consists of destroying the prison, of resolving the movement and of transcending the primordial silence itself.

If one is *attracted* by action or by qualities (which give impulse to action) or by principle-causal silence which resolves all and penetrates all, one is not ready to follow the "Pathway of Fire."

If one is *interred* in action, one is a slave to events; if one is urged by qualities then one is a slave of enjoyment;

if one is attracted by silence one is a prisoner of *Nirvana*, of bliss or of paradise.

55. The way to Ain Soph is the way of *denial* (of appearances) and of *affirmation* (of Ain Soph). It is a pathway of death and of awakening; it is a pathway of solitude, courage, and of understanding.

Many love to play with the powers, few love to dominate the powers, very, very few love to transcend the powers.

56. The lower triad is the flower, the intermediate triad is the stem, while the upper triad is the seed: the "Pathway of Fire" is the extinction or the solution of the *seed*.

A seed-principle is *one* of the *infinite* seeds that Ain Soph may project upon its limitless screen. A seed-principle, seen from the Ain Soph angle, is *cause*, prison, conditioning. The absolute reality is more than a simple seed-principle, however indefinite its vital expressions may be.

Whoever dwells in the seed-principle dwells upon the plane of necessity; whoever dwells in or, more appropriately, dissolves himself in Ain Soph, achieves total and absolute freedom.

True liberty is not freedom "to do," but it means being free "to do" or "not to do"—and this liberty can be found only in the metaphysical dimension.

In the lower triad "doing" commands the individual; in the central triad acting is directed (and one cannot but act); in the upper triad we are in the realm of "non action"; only upon the plane of Ain Soph are we totally free from the need to act or not to act.

57. In the lower triad we are governed by the law, in the intermediate triad we are the law, in the upper triad we are cause of the law, while in the Ain Soph one is above and

beyond every law; that is, one transcends the laws of being. Whoever is against the law, whoever is outside all laws, whoever violates the law is not in Ain Soph.

58. The *mind*, in its total extension may arrive at the prime cause, but if it wishes to go further it must stop because *That* (Ain Soph) cannot be a mentally perceived object but the fruit of *realization*.

The infinite does not proceed from a center, from a point, because it is without center and without point, but it projects a center-point which is called Kether.

The mind, if it resolves itself in the center-point, no longer produces "representative thought" because in the center-point subject and object both vanish.

If one "thinks oneself" as being center-unity, one falls into a grave error typical of minds that fail to grasp their own workings. The empirical mind can only *create an image* of the center-unity or principle point; *to be* point one must abandon volume, planes, and lines, one must resolve oneself in essence, one must not *think oneself* center. Many believe themselves or imagine themselves silence, but *are not* silence. Silence is the highest degree of realization upon the manifest plane.

One must distinguish between *imagining oneself* and *being*.

Every representation is always referred to something, but being is not referred to anything if not to itself insofar as it is pure being.

Behind every representation there is He who represents, and when He who represents does not represent any longer there is silence, there is being or consciousness without superimpositions or imaginings.

59. The imperfect and the perfect, the relative and the absolute, good and evil, lower and upper, are repre-

sentations of Hod which operates through "polar imagining."
It is not possible *to imagine* Ain Soph; it is only possible *to realize* It. It is easier to imagine than to realize, wherefore there are many who imagine Kether, Chokmah, and even Ain Soph.

Whoever follows the "Pathway of Fire" must abandon imagination, representation and conceptualization; he or she must die to all kinds of mental objectification with courage. The only law to follow is that which leads to freedom.

On the Road of Return one must *extinguish oneself* in order to truly be .

To quench the triple fire (triple triad) one requires maturity, dignity, daring and intuitive knowledge.

Whoever has quenched the triple fire—while still having a body—is a "living corpse" (*jivan-mukta* = living liberated one).

A "living corpse" leaves no tracks or traces; one has no *aims* to achieve, or *duties* to fulfill.

The fulfilled lives only of fulfillment and of fullness, and this fullness is free from all determination, from all action, from all purpose.

60. Tiphereth is universal understanding, it is vital harmony, it is also knowledge; therefore, it assumes the role of instructor but it must know how to find the daring and determination to cross the abyss without delay—not for individual reasons—into the world of "shadows."

Its flight toward Kether must be that of the swallow, without agitation or clamor; it must allow itself to be "attracted," it must glide without effort, without any resistance, into the One without motion.

During this flight that brings one higher and higher, and therefore toward the borders of the non-formal, one sees no "others." Words fail, thoughts cease, plans lose all meaning; there are no answers for anybody for, during this flight, the circumferences begin to fade, as one gradually discovers that nothing exists outside the Self.

In the flash of the rays of the polar Sun the "shadows" become clear, become limpid and dissolve into points without dimension.

With whom can one speak if there are no "others"?

With what can one think if there is no projective mind and, therefore, no problems to solve?

To whom can one "cling" if there is no second as support?

The "Pathway of Fire" is the way without support, without relationships, because the ultimate truth or reality rests only upon itself. The "Pathway of Fire" is the Pathway of the Strong, of those who dare to plunge into the nameless ocean, allowing themselves *to die* happily, to decompose, to depolarize like a pinch of salt that melts in water.

61. One instant of distraction is sufficient to find oneself looking downward again: thus, the "shadows" reappear, they stand out against the horizon-screen and the *motion of relation* involves one once more.

Some seem to be *ready* but they lack decision; that decision which is not desire or aspiration; it is not even will, it is something that stems from the awareness that the existing All does not exist.

There are no techniques at certain levels, nor are there philosophies, nor Gods to adore, nor energetic qualities to express. To "resolve oneself," one requires the dignity and awareness that are consubstantial to the being that has *comprehended*.

The Way of the Abyss is a way of rediscovery, of reintegration and revelation of true, supreme and boundless freedom.

62. Whoever loves freedom (not that of the ego-shadow) has no choice but to pursue the way of the Ain Soph; the Abyss awaits those who love that freedom which is peace and the sweetness of fulfillment. The Abyss is capable of shattering the chains that for long ages have bound human beings in a dimension of identification and bewilderment.

A Pathway of Fire which is capable of extinguishing desire for power and existence (both individual and universal) awaits those who love freedom; desire that—as a surrogate—tries desperately to compensate for that freedom which is the fruit of neither human nor divine projections.

Whosoever catches a glimpse of true liberty can no longer allow himself or herself to live in necessity, even if this belonged to the intermediate and upper triad.

Whoever loves absolute freedom from all kinds of deceiving dualism can allow no weakness, no hesitation, no delays, no alibis, however noble and praiseworthy.

Whoever loves freedom allows the triple world of necessity to burn itself out without regrets, without lamentations, without wonder: when the clear light of the Sun shines on the horizon, who on earth would dare to cling to the weak reflected light of the Moon?

What we call life is in fact death, necessity, and darkness; what we call death is freedom and fullness of being.

Binah is the creator of necessity but also of freedom; if one is capable of daring, the destructive fire of Binah may burn to ashes that life-death to which we cling so childishly on account of metaphysical ignorance.

If formal life is for the weak, to cling to the many bodily supports of life is for the weak, too, and so is the urge to preserve; to die consciously is for the strong, as for them is the task of quenching the fire that nourishes *qualities* and *corporality*.

Tiphereth, Kether, Ain Soph: this is the Way of Fire. Tiphereth as humble reflection must re-integrate with Kether; Kether as simple determination or as the point of Ain Soph, must *die* to itself and rediscover itself to be absolute liberty.

63. There are, at every level and degree, souls that descend, souls that keep what they have, and souls that lay down their load and, in courageous silence, choose the metaphysical way of the unqualified Infinite.

If Ain Soph is absolute reality and freedom without constraint, why therefore, should one fear? What can hold one back in the world of necessity?

There are souls that defend their own egoism, there are souls that defend their own "mission," their own disinterested action and their own *kṣatriya* requests (*kṣatriya* = order of law-givers and rulers), and there are other souls that dissolve themselves in metaphysical silence, having transcended every kind of doing and non-doing, of action and non-action, of being and non-being.

The Way of the Abyss is the Way of Silence; but, beware, *noise* might well re-attract one; those who were once our shadow-companions during the *fall* might offer us stimulating sophisms and cause us to fall again into imprisoning noise. One must be on one's guard; what for some is nourishment for others is poison.

64. What we prospect here is the way to Ain Soph, not that to Yesod or Malkuth; we propose the way of depolarization, not that of polarization; we are pointing toward the way of reintegration, not to that of extroversion and generation.

If the iron compound (mass) wishes to dissolve into energy it must attain silence and die to itself (as the element iron).

The Pathway of Return is the way of *solution*, of *dispersion*, of *demagnetization*. The Pathway of Return is the way of maturity, conversion, and detachment. But it is not the way of abandonment, flight, or opposition. It is a good thing to reflect upon this fact.

65. Knowledge is a thirst for truth, love is a thirst for union-identity, will is a thirst for being; Ain Soph is beyond knowing, loving and willing.

66. We shall now re-propose what has been said about *Asparsa yoga*,[10] the pure metaphysical *yoga*, because we feel that it is relevant to the pathway to Ain Soph.

According to Meyerson, human beings practice metaphysics just as easily as they breathe, without minding it.[11]

The spontaneous need to transcend and create for oneself goals that are beyond one's own fleeting dimen-

---

[10]See the translation from the Sanskrit and notes by Raphael of Mandukya Upanishad with Gaudapada's Karikas and Samkara's Commentary (Rome, Italy: Edizioni Āśram Vidyā, 1976), p. 18f.

[11]Emile Meyerson (Lublino 1859-Paris 1933) was a French philosopher of Polish hebraic origin. His main works include: *Identité et réalité; De l'explication dans les sciences; La deduction relativiste; Du cheminement de la pensée.*

sion is innate in human nature. Metaphysics was born with the cosmos, itself, because every particle of the universe tends toward its total existential reintegration.

Human beings are restless, and have always been compelled to surpass themselves, or rather, to go beyond their natural condition, to achieve a "beyond" that is often difficult to define, but which represents, in actual fact, denial or refusal of all limitations and, therefore, of the finite composite world of appearances.

According to Descartes, the secret of the method consists in seeking, with the utmost care, that which is most absolute in all things.

The need of the absolute is a prime necessity for the human mind, which implies that in all orders of reality there must be a prime term (*adhi*) which is the condition of all the rest (and, as such, independent, at least within its own order) and which, in the strictest sense, may be considered absolute and the only absolute without a second.

One should notice that the philosophy (especially modern and Western philosophy), which contests the capacity to discover the absolute, merely transfers to the world of sensorial experience the character of absoluteness.

The metaphysician pursues the straight road of integral awareness and cognitive reintegration into the absolute being from which all emanates and proceeds. Rather than take an interest in the world of phenomena and structure, rather than see how the "object-universe" is made, how its laws and its magical and deforming phenomena work, rather than acquire formal power, the metaphysician points toward the a-principial absolute being or the non-being, toward the undifferentiated, the ineffable, the unknowable (through the senses).

Metaphysics is interested in what is "beyond the physical," beyond nature, beyond gross and subtle forms, beyond the substantial, beyond the principle One itself, beyond the God-Person; beyond all objectivity and subjectivity, beyond all possible polarity. This implies that metaphysics deals with the absolute, the constant, the infinite, non-being as pure and only being, the unconditioned, the one-without-a-second (*advaita*). Metaphysics goes beyond the physical, the psychic, the spiritual. What is related to the individual, and therefore to the general, concerns science; what is related to the universal—Transcendental Unity or Totality—regards metaphysics.

If metaphysics is a quest for the absolute or reality without a second, then it cannot be schematized, conceptualized or placed within any individualized mental framework. The absolute or supreme reality cannot be circumscribed, represented or brought upon the plane of empirical relativism, nor can it be considered the exclusive property of an individual or a people.

To achieve metaphysical realization certain qualities are undoubtedly required—first of all, a mind capable of synthesis and of grasping the a-temporal. Most people are enslaved by time-space-causality and, in actual fact, it is very difficult to break free of it, but if one wishes to realize metaphysical knowledge one must *fly*, one must bring oneself beyond time and space, beyond the contingent, the individual and the general; in other words, one must learn to remain *without support*. From this comes the name *asparsa* which means non-contact, without relations, without rapport, without support. Therefore one must also pay appropriate attention to this fact, because we are in the presence of a very particular and special type of knowledge which does not act according to the rules of ordinary discoursive or empirical knowledge. This is the true "Pathway of Fire" because at its touch all *maya*'s objective possibilities are burned and because the entity reveals and shows itself in all its self-splendor. To grasp a-temporality in its immediacy means not depending upon any empirical kind of *yoga* practice or upon any type of psycho-physical exercise; it means suddenly immersing oneself in the all-inclusive and all-pervading present. Metaphysical realization can be implemented by means of that particular kind of mind which we might define as *mens informalis.*

The difficulty in grasping the absolute is great because it is not with the mind, which operates within the realm of subject-object, that one can understand non-duality. Vain are the efforts of those who try to consider the absolute as a simple *object* of mental representation. One might say that *asparsa*, in order to be truly understood, necessarily and unequivocally imposes an identity approach. In other words, being a *yoga* without relationships, it is, obviously and above all, a *yoga* without supports. Thus one must place oneself immediately within the Self, without leaning upon external objects or individual qualifications, such as feeling, wishing, or empirical knowing.

The other kinds of *yoga* necessarily require aspiration, a vertical thrust, and an impulse that stem from individuality as effect, and aim at transcending individuality itself; these types of *yoga*, therefore, require desire. Upon the pure metaphysical pathway it is no longer desire that determines what occurs, but awareness of "finding oneself," of being. The disciple is not pushed, he or she is held back; one might say that he or she is not compelled toward the acquisition of something (whether of the upper or the lower order), but toward the resolution of every request of *maya*, including that of union in the ordinary sense.

The disciple of *asparsa yoga* withdraws and comprehends the absolute, which unfolds itself in all its majesty within the secret recesses of his or her heart. Beyond all ideas, concepts, idols, phenomena, there is *That*, which is totality, not subject to or dependent upon any concept or change. The "metaphysically reintegrated" have the privilege and the power to see all the phenomena of life in the light of the metaphysical zero.

Asparsa yoga leads to liberation, or better still, to active reintegration (in actual fact, one cannot speak even of liberation in the case of this type of *yoga*) and realizes that sole, undifferentiated, uncreated or a-causal unmanifest and impersonal essence from which the whole object-universe, as a chain of *maya* perceptions of light, sprung. Being *is*, and one cannot add anything further, because to say that being is "this or that" means that being *is not*. To go on maintaining that it may be something other than what it is means stating that at the same time a datum both *is* and *is not*. Besides, if being has "become" this or that, then it must have come from a being or from a non-being. If it comes from a non-being, then one states an absurdity because nothing is ever created from nothing; if it comes from being, then we must agree that being stems from being, which means that it remains constantly equal to itself in all its indivisibility and, in that case, one cannot speak of becoming or of birth or of finding oneself in another condition, because being that remains identical to itself does not undergo any movement, any birth, or any change.

One requires a certain type of understanding (not of the sensorial order) to consider that what is universal, absolute, a-formal cannot be transposed into any particular dialectical perspective, or into any kind of dogmatic rationalism. The metaphysical pathway stands upon the plane of informal intelligence and the emotional sphere is completely excluded from it. This type of *yoga* is the *yoga* of pure intuition of things and of appearances; it goes beyond all phenomenology, all common reason, all kinds of religion, all changeable social morality, all sensorial experience, as all these things are the outcome of mediated knowledge. The metaphysical truth has no scheme, concept or mental, analytical framework because it transcends all physical experience. On the other hand, to meditate upon what does not correspond to any sensorial datum is not easy; the sensorial mind needs to conceive all reality in relation to a form, an image, and most of the time the image itself imprisons the thinker who, on the contrary, should always be independent. The metaphysical pathway presents certain difficulties because one must abandon normal thinking processes and transfer oneself into a condition of a-dimensional, a-formal, unusual understanding. This, obviously, requires abandoning the personal and collective unconscious.

A premature approach to this pathway might well paralyze the normal perceptive and sensorial thinking process, without leading to superior understanding. The result would be endless mental inertia and confusion with aberrant states of consciousness giving rise to the annihilation of representative mental dynamics. This danger can be more acute in the West because here one tends to have a sensorial-formal kind of mind to which unique and irreplaceable values are attributed. The metaphysical way is certainly the road which *comprehends* the Infinite with its manifesting and manifest virtual possibilities. This *comprehension* is integral Realization in that the adept has realized an effective, conscious (not theoretical) identity (because in that case knowledge would be simply of the sensorial or rational-formal order, therefore mere erudition), which is not virtual because such a condition has always existed and has never ceased to exist. One does not arrive at *asparsa yoga* by means of self-imposed discipline, by faith, devotion or any kind of action due to individual-sensorial expression, but through a deeply interior kind of self-awareness where all extroverted energy tends to exhaust itself, rendering the spirit totally *free*. Once the undivided point has been reached, the notion of translatory movement no longer exists; the *spirit*, by eliminating the form, or its own reflection being quenched, returns to its essence, devoid of cause, time and space.

Asparsa yoga represents the last step. It is the goal of all experience and human realizational possibility. Beyond all experience there is a "moment" of total comprehension of our own essence; it is the maturity of perfect equilibrium and preexistential a-condition. The ordinary individual is bound by concepts of time and space, therefore to the manifested, to the evolving object; only very few are capable of revealing that eternal present, that *alpha* and *omega* of what is commonly called change. The metaphysician, not satisfied with having transcended the limited world of subject-object, dares to climb up onto the last informal step of the vibrating universal stairway to... discover himself or herself.

Asparsa yoga may be considered the highest expression of spiritual knowledge, a kind of knowledge or understanding by identity that integrally leads from the unreal to the real, from death to life, from the finite to the infinite, from the relative (human and divine) to the unqualified absolute without a second, from illusory differentiation to supreme identity.

Index